OTAKAR ŠEVČÍK Opus 3

Forty Variations
for Viola arranged by

Vierzig Variationen
für Viola bearbeitet von

Quarante Variations
arrangées pour alto par

Margaret Major

Preface

So that this Opus can be played with the existing Piano accompaniment, I have kept to the original keys, except for the last three Variations, which are transcribed a fifth down from the Violin version.

M.M.

Vorwort

Damit auch in dieser Viola-Ausgabe der vorhandene Klavierpart als Begleitung verwendet werden kann, habe ich die Original-Tonarten beibehalten. Hiervon ausgenommen sind lediglich die letzten drei Variationen, die gegenüber der Ausgabe für Violine um eine Quinte nach unten versetzt wurden.

M.M.

Préface

Afin que cet opus puisse être joué avec l'accompagnement de piano existant, j'ai conservé les tonalités originales sauf pour les trois dernières variations qui sont transcrites une quinte en dessous de la version pour violon.

M.M.

Margaret Major is Professor of Viola at the Royal College of Music, London. The first recipient of the Lionel Tertis Prize, she was Principal Viola of the Netherlands Chamber Orchestra and later of the Philomusica of London. From 1965-1981, she was the Violist of the Aeolian String Quartet.

Margaret Major ist Dozentin für Bratsche am Royal College of Music in London. Als erste wurde sie mit dem Lionel-Tertis-Preis ausgezeichnet, sie war Prim-Bratschistin im Kammerorchester der Niederlande und später bei der Londoner Philomusica. Von 1965 bis 1981 gehörte ihr der Platz als Bratschistin im Aeolian String Quartett.

Margaret Major est professeur d'alto au College Royal de Musique de Londres. Elle reçut le prix Lionel Tertis, fut alto principal de l'Orchestre de Chambre Néerlandaise et plus tard du Philomusica de Londres. De 1965 à 1981, elle fut l'altiste de l'Aeolian String Quartet.

Cover picture: an important viola by Giovanni Paolo Maggini, c.1600-1610. Photograph from Christie's of London.

Bosworth

Forty Variations Op. 3
by Otakar Ševčík

Vierzig Variationen Op. 3
von Otakar Ševčík

Quarante Variations Op. 3
par Otakar Ševčík

VIOLA — ALTO

arranged by/bearbeitet von/arrangées par Margaret Major

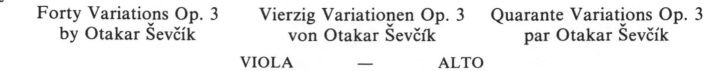

Tema.

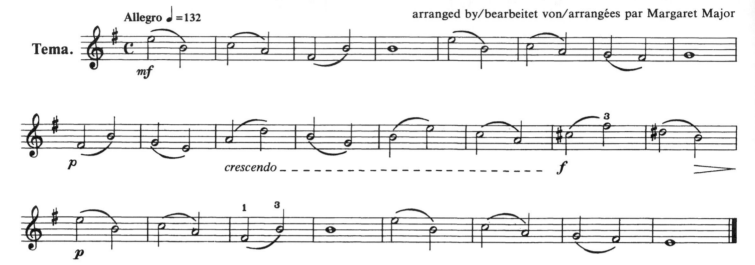

Var. 1.

B. & Co. Ltd. 22256

4

B. & Co. Ltd. 22256

8

VERÄNDERUNGEN
DES BOGENSTRICHES

ALSO WITH
THESE BOWINGS

CHANGEMENTS
DES COUPS D'ARCHET

Var. 14. Allegro ♩=152

Var. 15. Allegretto ♩.=63

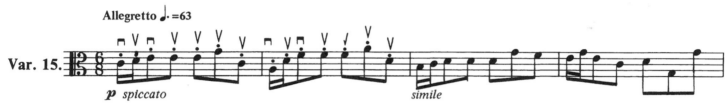

12

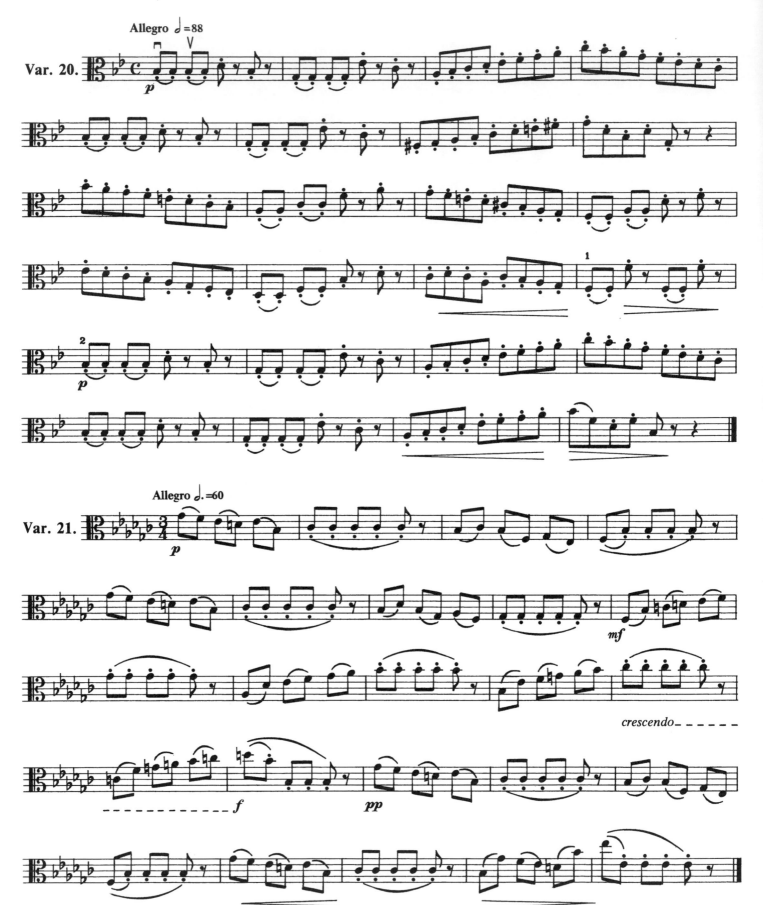

13

VERÄNDERUNGEN
DES BOGENSTRICHES

ALSO WITH
THESE BOWINGS

CHANGEMENTS
DES COUPS D'ARCHET

B. & Co. Ltd. 22256

VERÄNDERUNGEN
DES BOGENSTRICHES

ALSO WITH
THESE BOWINGS

CHANGEMENTS
DES COUPS D'ARCHET

Allegretto ♩=104

Var. 33.

dolce

crescendo   mf

pizz.

Allegro ♩=126

Var. 34.

spiccato

B. & Co. Ltd. 22256

22

**VERÄNDERUNGEN
DES BOGENSTRICHES**

**ALSO WITH
THESE BOWINGS**

**CHANGEMENTS
DES COUPS D'ARCHET**

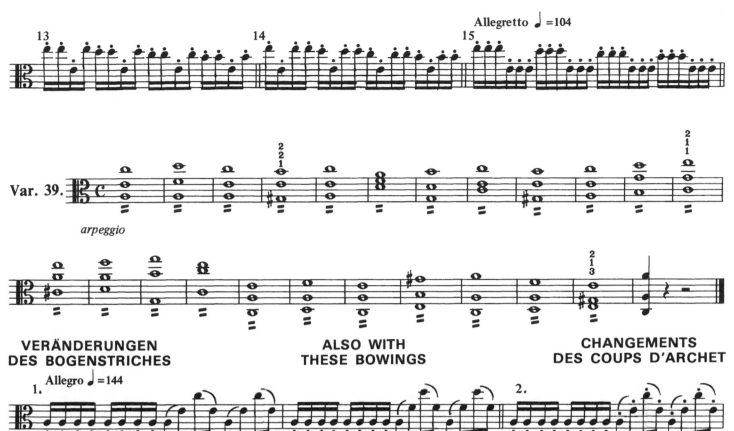

VERÄNDERUNGEN DES BOGENSTRICHES   **ALSO WITH THESE BOWINGS**   **CHANGEMENTS DES COUPS D'ARCHET**

23

Var. 39.

arpeggio

24

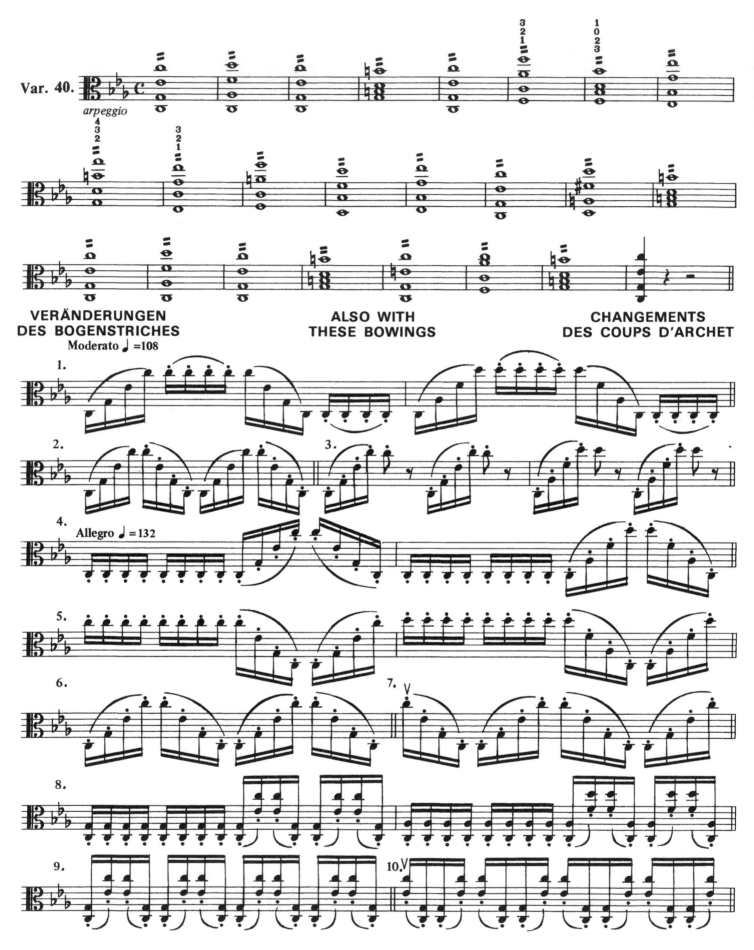

VERÄNDERUNGEN DES BOGENSTRICHES

ALSO WITH THESE BOWINGS

CHANGEMENTS DES COUPS D'ARCHET

B. & Co Ltd. 22256